A Visit to the Museum

by Rosalyn Clark

BUMBA BOOKS™

LERNER PUBLICATIONS ◆ MINNEAPOLIS

Note to Educators:

Throughout this book, you'll find critical thinking questions. These can be used to engage young readers in thinking critically about the topic and in using the text and photos to do so.

Lerner Publications Company
A division of Lerner Publishing Group, Inc.
241 First Avenue North
Minneapolis, MN 55401 USA

For reading levels and more information, look up this title at www.lernerbooks.com.

Library of Congress Cataloging-in-Publication Data

Names: Clark, Rosalyn, 1990– author.
Title: A visit to the museum / by Rosalyn Clark.
Description: Minneapolis : Lerner Publications, 2018. | Series: Bumba books. Places we go | Includes bibliographical references and index.
Identifiers: LCCN 2016045735 (print) | LCCN 2016050737 (ebook) | ISBN 9781512433715 (library bound alkaline paper) | ISBN 9781512455632 (paperback : alkaline paper) | ISBN 9781512450453 (eb pdf)
Subjects: LCSH: Museums—Juvenile literature. | Museum exhibits—Juvenile literature.
Classification: LCC AM7 .C568 2018 (print) | LCC AM7 (ebook) | DDC 069—dc23

LC record available at https://lccn.loc.gov/2016045735

Manufactured in the United States of America
1—CG—7/15/17

Expand learning beyond the printed book. Download free, complementary educational resources for this book from our website, www.lernerresource.com.

Table of Contents

Time for a Field Trip

It is time for a class field trip!

We get on a bus.

We are going to a museum.

The museum is huge!

We meet our guide.

She shows us around.

There are many exhibits.

There is so much to learn!

What kinds of exhibits do you think museums have?

We see fossils.

Look at that dinosaur fossil!

Some dinosaurs had big teeth.

Why do you think museums have fossils?

We learn about

ocean animals.

We see bones from whales.

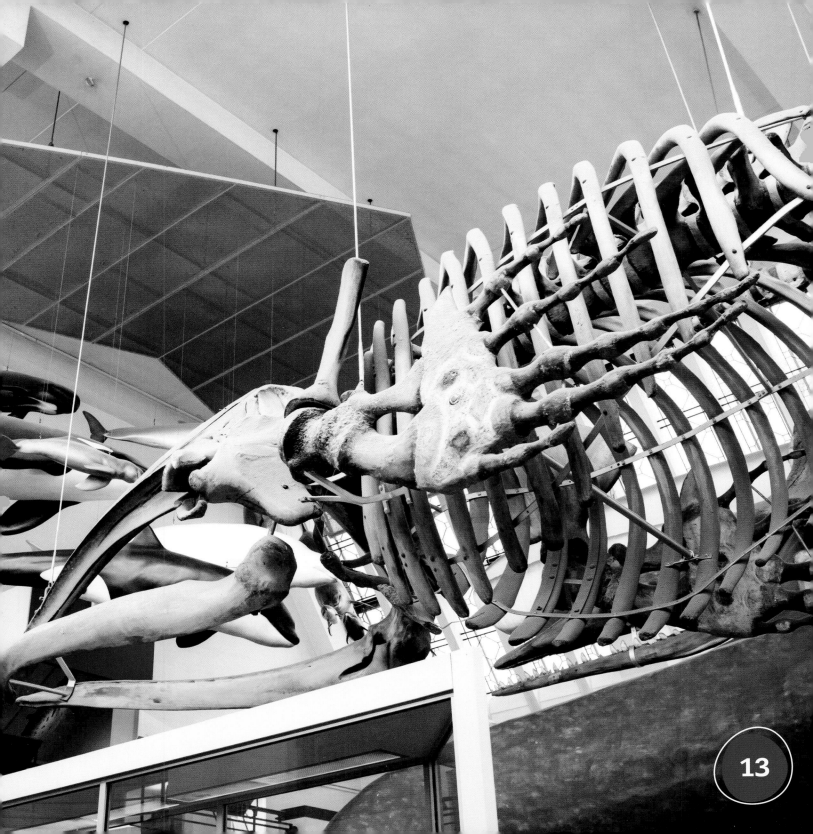

One exhibit is about Asia.

We see a leopard.

Leopards live in Asia.

We learn about the country of Egypt. We see mummies. They are thousands of years old.

What other old things might you see at a museum?

We see art from many

parts of the world.

We see colorful masks.

They are from

South America.

There are many things to see

at a museum!

Would you like to visit a museum?

What to See at a Museum

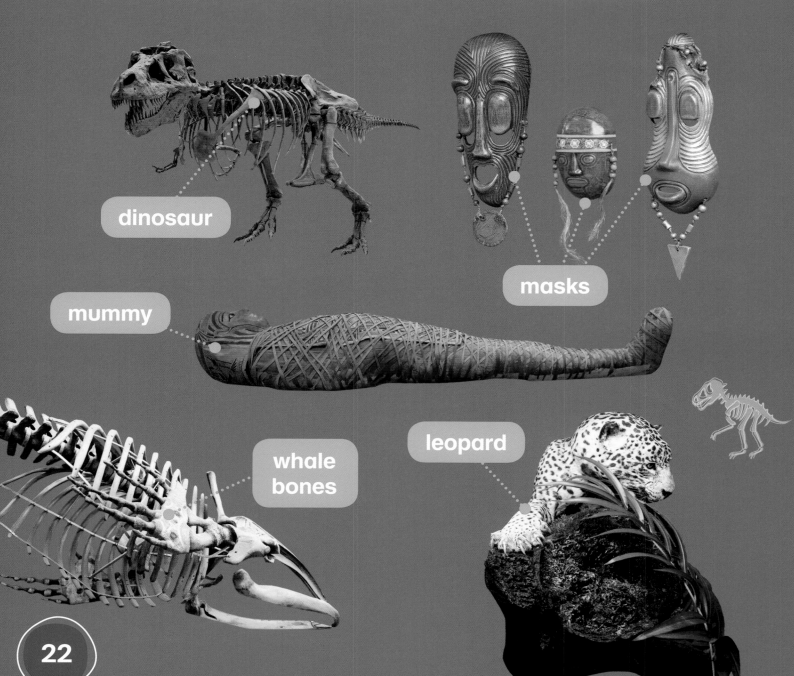

dinosaur

masks

mummy

whale bones

leopard

Picture Glossary

exhibits

rooms that have objects on display for people to see

fossils

bones or other pieces of an animal from long ago that have turned to rock

guide

a person who shows and explains things in a museum

mummies

bodies that Egyptians prepared for burial

23

Read More

Bishop, Celeste. *A Day at the Children's Museum.* New York: PowerKids, 2017.

Kim, Yu-ri. *Fossils Tell Stories.* Minneapolis: Big & Small, 2015.

Rober, Harold T. *Triceratops.* Minneapolis: Lerner Publications, 2017.

Index

Photo Credits